Silver River Library

P9-AGN-100

tar
S

RECEIVED

JUL 1 0 2018

david
martin

tar
swan

POEMS

NEWEST PRESS

COPYRIGHT © DAVID MARTIN 2018

All rights reserved. The use of any part of this publication — reproduced, transmitted in any form or by any means, electronic, mechanical, recording or otherwise, or stored in a retrieval system — without the prior consent of the publisher is an infringement of the copyright law. In the case of photocopying or other reprographic copying of the material, a licence must be obtained from Access Copyright before proceeding.

Library and Archives Canada Cataloguing in Publication
Martin, David, 1982–, author
Tar swan / David Martin.
(Crow said poetry series)
Poems.
Issued in print and electronic formats.
ISBN 978-1-988732-18-3 (softcover).   ISBN 978-1-988732-19-0 (epub).
ISBN 978-1-988732-20-6 (Kindle)
I. Title.
PS8626.A76945T37 2018   C811'.6   C2017-905192-X   C2017-905193-8

Board editor: Jenna Butler
Book design: Natalie Olsen, Kisscut Design
Cover texture: Eky Studio / Shutterstock.com
Author photo: James Levy

Excerpt from THE METAMORPHOSES OF OVID: A New Verse Translation, translated by Allen Mandelbaum. English translation copyright © 1993 by Allen Mandelbaum. Reprinted by permission of Houghton Mifflin Harcourt Publishing Company. All rights reserved.

"The Truth About Alberta Tar Sands" by R.C. Fitzsimmons was accessed by the author on July 22, 2017 at http://www.history.alberta.ca/energyheritage/bitumount/the-people/promoters-and-politicians/robert-cosmas-fitzsimmons/the-truth-about-alberta-tar-sands.aspx and is in the public domain.

NeWest Press acknowledges the support of the Canada Council for the Arts, the Alberta Foundation for the Arts, and the Edmonton Arts Council for support of our publishing program. This project is funded in part by the Government of Canada.

201, 8540 – 109 Street
Edmonton, AB T6G 1E6
780.432.9427
www.newestpress.com

NeWest Press

No bison were harmed in the making of this book.
Printed and bound in Canada   1 2 3 4 5   20 19 18

To honour NeWest Press' 40th anniversary, we've inaug-
urated a new poetry series to go alongside our Nunatak
First Fiction, Prairie Play, and Writer as Critic series:
Crow Said Poetry. Crow Said is named in honour of Robert
Kroetsch's foundational 1977 novel *What The Crow Said*.
The series has as its aim to shed light on places and people
outside of the literary mainstream. It is our intention
that the poets featured in this series will continue Robert
Kroetsch's literary tradition of innovation, interrogation,
and generosity of spirit.

for
Marsha

He starts to strip his foe, and then he sees
that underneath the armor there's no body;
for Cycnus had acquired a new form:
the sea-god changed him into the white swan
whose name the Phrygian had already borne.

OVID

we had reason to believe that the cause
of the trouble was by design...

RCF

ROBERT C. FITZSIMMONS (top and bottom of page, block text):
First man to unveil a commercial oil sands separation plant.
He poses, hands clasped, on a boulder by the Athabaska river.

FRANK BADURA (top of page, broken text):
Plant mechanic accused by Fitzsimmons of sabotage.
He kneels by the boiler.

DR. BRIAN K. WOLSKY (top of page, two-line stanzas):
Archaeologist excavating prehistoric sites and the historic
Fitzsimmons camp. He stratifies himself in a pit.

SWAN (middle of page):
Ignored by the others, wading ashore.

I was born a single cygnet, ditched
by Cob and Pen, left fending
in quickening lichen like mud-coaxed
bastard oxen, as shredded elephants
choired from their soup. Do not blotch
brittle leaves with tears, for my sobs,
skip-dripping from sockets, slithered
thence to the ground and pooled deep
pockets of felicity. Doodle-buggers
and orange-worms mine a blistered delight.
My feathers and feces drive your cars:
inquire of coke-drowned patch clowns
who pray for forgiveness, quitting town.

Edmonton's money is a locked fist, Manning's door knows the heat of my breath, and his secretary is a smiling hell-dog. Each morning I challenge him, and Frank nods that, yes, the men are sole-held, that this gaggle of meat cannot assume a single thought. But how long can I swear by him — I don't need to name skull-diggers again. How long can this live, without a cusp of tomorrow's sunlight? I have collected your telegrams, but you know as well as I this is no loam for a woman. The boreal's a brute, not a carpet to set your baby toe upon, Wilhelmina. — RCF

I start'd a scow mule

forty long to McMurray
for which? whiskey pant

guy-line-notch'd shoulders

squeezed his spiel
and swell'd
to blot my name

for Fitz says he'll pay on the reg'lar
fine line by me

Gentlemen, how many Snakes did you cook today?
How much Caragana stubbles your hair? How weary
of sky's Dominion? How many Cotter Bolts swindle
your shoes? How many birch leaves Coil at your neck?
How can you let this sharpen? Witness Robert C.
Fitzsimmons steering you today. I offer an opportunity
to Tickle, with your own eyes, the Tail of Charybdis.
I offer the Belly beneath Bitumount's bloody baby toe.
I give you (between us men) three angels: a senator,
a nameless investor, and a Karl Clark, all failing to
out-swim my sequinned Undertow.

last spring
Danny
drown'd
in his tar pool —
dangling
sugar-shack man

I swear to Judas
ducks were haw-hawing us
from their frittering perch

spent three days paring planks
for Fitz's boiler

beets drum the plates
and bleed into meats

Gentlemen, say Alexander Mackenzie once netted an Elephant by the jugular, a vein he blotted ashore, and ashore he cajoled a catheter up its trunk, a trunk that smelled of sea coal. Believe me, he never imagined his mammoth-heir would become Nature's Supreme Gift to Industry and tender its body as Petroleum, Plastics, Post Preserver, Pitch, Printer's Ink, Proof Paint, Patent Leather, Pressure Pipes, Primer, Power Pumps, and Palliative Medicine for Poor Skin. We are Bitumen Bloodmen, and sloop-borne we scud with the wide plough, a plough leaving ragged furrow-waves in our coulter's wake. Wake, and never again will Virgil warn, let the horns of the moon govern a Soiler's work!

Window-bunked, and a different plant blinks the night. Illuminated, its rigid stalk and dandy branches ratchet soil, like Dante's damned twigs growing upside down. Leaves snatch my room from a hole with spits of light, throwing up against the wall my sad-sack cot, before withering back into cloud. Sleep, and a season's worth will grow and wilt against the sky — that strange mirror of midnight earth, churned by worms mining to morning, Wilhelmina. — RCF

we wade the same bed
each day

not much to brain-fancy
towing a sin of cores
against th' Athabaska

cutthroat trout
chain'd to my ankles

Luther broke to brush

Adam lapsed
and we interred
him — somewhere

least Fitz keeps my baby
toe free from water fits

Slipshod Athabaska is my barouche,
currying zombie currents that I may
syphon the gaze of One: Darling
Fitzy. His ants, a turbulent tableaux
on Bitumount's bald shore. I busk
flags, herald the stained egg
nesting in dollmoss, girdled with
deer skin. He alights on my lore;
I crack the sootseed, spit into yoke,
shake cocktail under his fluted lips
and pour pure soup over forehead.
He babbles a tar-cleaned tongue,
as I yaw and observe the fun.

A gaggle of hired meat doesn't gawk
when I un-skin for a dip, my sail
slung on a jack-pine coatstand. Behold
the billies, strewing themselves to boil
and skim, as Fitzy unveils Plant, his
mask's Augustan shine clodhopper-cast.
He feathers cheeks, declaims tide and tide
again what we've consummated.
But I crack black omelettes as souvenirs
of whence eleemosynary shit comes.
He beats my glances off, primps for
the hooded cameraman, but my mirror's
so tight it stuns him with a mickle twin.

As I slept, a creature brewed before me: head a white-tongued lion, body the blood of a cinnamon hermit, feet the sheaths of a fire moth — and as I pounced, flailing hands, hurling clods of shadow-sand in its mask, trying to bite out eyes — nothing would injure the monster, no wound appeared anywhere on craning form. At last, I filled its throat with heavy stones, stuffing a gaunt neck, peeled back layers of rotted cloak to find brittle feathers, no bulk beneath, but a single black egg taken up. A black egg wrapped in moss, my Wilhelmina. — RCF

Gentlemen, we must, as I've pleaded, tide and tide again, we must alight beneath the ground, as our calling requires perfection of sustenance — Bodies Be Minds. These stumps anchor their loam-rust within our home pools, fouling our future stock. We must unlock their spoiled hold over us thusly: MOCK the many dour stubs, BAIT tap root with stomps, tea-cup TRENCH the trunk, EVICT and SCANDAL roots, HACK hairy tentacles, DRAIN the body from bed, POSE seed potatoes, and, at last, DOUSE ourselves with Gin. Gin for our Bodies Be Minds!

45–30 cm, below
one retouched split chert pebble

We eat and sleep in pits, grave
teasing, as canny strata shirk

the dune's heat, and Prof. sips
library gin back in Edmonton.

Athabasca blares behind a butte.
Lafont butts the current's nap.

Dusty cumulus-bergs drift,
scrape dirty feet on grounds.

One hundred pieces of shatter
can be patched,

he would say, revealing a fluted
point cast in light and air.

Gentlemen, Sunday-surrender to body whims and shilly-shally Yourselves with a harvest of plate colour. Feet high, smoke over Northern Fortune about to sink our Knickerbockers. London's Capital is train-bound for our Boilers. We swat away Comers with our Coffer, desperate for our Second Line swig. Edmonton's toil tires smooth over our Proof and Profit. Karl Clark jewels in surprise at my Wrought-Iron Spires. But keep the specs fast, My Billies. Shun slippage. Rust wretches, any schemers stripping our Prize. Set the watch to tattoo, for tomorrow is tomorrow and tide is tiding again.

45–30 cm, below
two end scrapers

The bulb of percussion:
petrified swan egg.

Now trace a striated map,
conchoidal fractures

knocked by a knapper
who curve-cut random

radiating waves, blows still
echoing in obsidian ears.

Thirty days of tuna sandwiches.
Thirty days of scrub chatter.

Prof. Jenkins's rippling laugh
could talk your heart off.

Deracinated from maternal waters,
I struck out to parley with past-mongers
who squire in puzzle-cut earth, reading
the old news for new. Poor sods, they
sift debitage my randy brain sabotaged
by casting Cadmus table scraps
among the midden mines. Look at them
scrooch to ponder shards I disseminated
after imbibing an injudicious slug
of river shine. My webs were toppled
when I tea-kettled over root thugs,
but I slept it off, serenaded by sunskirl,
prodding the dunes of fuggy Fort Hills.

Gentlemen, now that we've sailed this far, I can leak a Secret bestowed upon me, and me alone, by Dr. Karl A. Clark, Diviner Extraordinaire: "Every Magician knows the Stubholder's double watch: convincing Heart that behind the Trick is Trick, hoodwinking Body-Be-Mind to lunch with Wonder. It's simple, then: Threshing Bitumen is the Devil's Handkerchief followed by a Question of Sympathy. Suckers agog, exposed by Boreal Thugs who conjure terrible Prophecies, stringing out a Dionysian Muck to smear on Highway Blacktop. Finally, by sleight-of-hand, they sluice foaming Shades from the Body, as the Stage Manager skins his take, scuttles applause." I saw it Myself, but my Eyes would not. I tell It now, as if Your ears will.

Fitz blew in the mess
gifting us a shortwave

this man Orson Welles
is Shadow

some gangster's gun
is scrubbing the room
for a voice

bullet caught Shadow's belly

wound dangling midair
as if wing'd

Again the plant hives at twilight, machinery excreting without me. Manning, Clark, all bees at eyes, cast in brood-comb wax, regurgitated nectar under breath. In my sleep I cut out my tongue, only dancing the figure eight, shake, plume belly stink, silver toe, Lindy whisk, breakaway gancho, until Jim puts my arms back on and crutches the rays into my sockets, my dear Wilhelmina. — RCF

45–30 cm, below
lithic core

I syphon from sour soil
a bifurcated chunk of high-art.

Scalloped scars mark
how trimming flakes

sprayed from platform,
beaten out of bedding.

Waste shrinks as the hand
cleaves closer to heart.

I, too, can talk down a spark
to hew a blade

from its cradle, then scrape fat
off a mottled moon-skin.

Saw the new doc in McMurray today, who ogled my feet, haranguing "how a man's middle name and shoes betray his disorders. Sagging inner contour: pancake paw. Worn lateral border: plantar effigy. Wan toes: foot coop. Broken tongue: talon traitor. Pruned outer sole: pigeon ham. Oblique creases: tough-nut claw-off, Achilles, asunder." At last, I pronounce, "Cosmas," and he retreats until I can see his skunk eye, my Wilhelmina. — RCF

30–25 cm, below
workshop debitage

History sauntered away
through Fort Hills' ditches.

Bifaces, scrapers, chert shatter
shed by nomadic midden-makers.

Never resurrect unburnt bone.
Ticking from our deadwood tripod,

interrogated dirt goes through
our screens: Six slate pencils,

two fruit pits, one porcelain saucer,
and the knapper's signature flute

that guttered a Clovis point —
my crew left tongue-struck.

Night-sluice this foaming pitch to
cauldron. In the jack-pine scrum,
skim cinder's cream and tender
before his door. I played skin
games in my youth, crawled inside
others for a tide. But Zeus once
carjacked my shell for a joyride
on Leda: two sets of unwilling limbs
tied in the thunderthresh of his thighs.
My feathered skin sighed, sighed.
A curse of matryoshka-doll ways:
the Cloud-Gatherer restored my husk,
still slicked with her smeared screams.

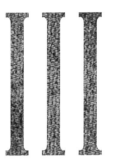

Poor Karl's skull pitty-pat-slapped
sideways, spilling a terrible tantrum.
I did court him with plumes, yes,
busked us to saloons till dawn. Oh, I
always try too hard to not help, whether
sharpening Gesualdo's sword to score
madrigals in his faithless wife, or
castrating Handel's batch of canters,
then goading God to break the Babel,
and tickling Van Gogh's ear as he tocked.
No man can resist a succulent neck,
nudging him toward rapture. Karl tunes
the ribs of his cage now, thumbs a brain.

Gentle Wilhelmina, a month ago I noticed a black bear at camp's edge. He'd turn up at seven each morning, pace by the settling tank's belly, and loll in pitch to deter flies. Strange to say, but one day I shot this poor beast, as it looked so much like you. Deciding I might as well open it up and have a look, I crawled inside before you could say "Hammerstein." Jim was aghast, but soon enough didn't seem to worry, and I felt quite at home. I kept it on day and dark, quickly forgot myself. As I'm sure you're aware, though, things like this begin to deteriorate, and I sloughed it off a piece at a time. I've never felt so naked as I do now. I spend most days shivering in shirtsleeves, vowels streaming from my mouth. —RCF

Gentlemen, we have arisen, our foes flee before us, and our enemies scatter. Behold, the Plant is alive! I give you the loafing-crunch of Draglined Sand; the shut-eye-beak-oool of Feed Hopper; the scheming-sheaths of Toothed Rollers; the rumen-torque of Pug Mill; the pupa-soup-gyrate of Separator; the moulted-scales of Tailings Pond; the magpie-appraisal of Settling Tank; the shadow-tailed-cache of Elephant Storage; the nagging-scent of Water Drained to River. Above all, I submit Nature's Supreme Gift to Industry! DOUSE ourselves with gin. Gin for our Bodies Be Minds!

Lloyd the fresh-clod
hack'd stumps
eight hours

blade talk'd
his flapper off
left him
in a war of trumpets

until we pinned him
to cauterize
the axed limb

me?
my lopsided bed makes
like I'm sleeping
on the edge of a kiln

30–25 cm, below
wood pith segments

These are beds, not
rank bog butter.

They tuck old things in,
keep spruce gagged.

We awoke a long bole
full of leeching clay.

The ripped roots loll
and rust at breath.

Feral stone resents
the heat of my hand,

but touch-hungry wood
swoons into a thousand fans.

Gentlemen, it is my burden to announce that our Friend and Champion within the Government's flooded circles, Karl Clark, has slipped beyond the Tides. His final letter, thus: *Forty years ago I bored the river flanks with my hand-auger, cataloguing core samples while the crew, my impedimenta, cowered in brush. As I paved the City of Edmonton, bureaucrats wouldn't dare my eyes, so burned reports each evening. Soon after, the dust began to collate. Today I pace my homestead, dictating currents that coat the world, behind my back. This wafting wake is a living record of microscopic stenographers. With my voice unencumbered by stops or pressure — plosive dam of catch, hold, and burst; fricative's narrow straits — the vowels are free to stream from mouth.* Clark, our Treading Ally, has let his Body-Be-Mind rot, and a Saboteur may even be skulking My Plant from within. No matter, Dear Friends, as I've told you time and tide again: Our Cause is our Own; we face them Alone.

With freetime to drown, Frank sidles
shorewise to skunkeye my scraw-stuffed
flutes. I prop my tar-kissed mantle
on his shoulder, hang over ears
and peck up his mealy torso. Frank
frets at my feet, shrieks at bolts eking
over floorboards, hamfists boiler,
and stumps the stippled stubble as I
take on his hair. Swan-man undercard,
feather-graze head, supervising slouch
and an unmade bed. Then I brood
on pink elephants, gulp bone slurry,
trill kin-brethren like an aphasic flapper.

Cora's letter knock'd —
things frozen again

my mind a well bucket
dripping drops
that make me *me*

Gary chants "Her tears
come down
like fallin' frogs"

I have to guzzle
to not get full-drown'd

20–15 cm, below
fifty-seven sheared cotter-pin bolts

Some with shattered dreams, cast off
on the run and divorced from hairpins

that held up curls. Fitzsimmons force-fed
ribbons to pug mills all midnight,

their thread crumbs turning to soot.
From the ember-blistered ground,

I brush up a glass eye,
its pupil preaching in my palm.

A master painted its iris-pond,
stroked with grit and silk veins.

This eye and I will unclothe the lives
vainly disguised by a fipple's keening.

10–5 cm, below
two slate pencils

Fitzsimmons slipped his typewriter
the same backing sheet

behind each bleached recto.
It braced against blows

from smut-footed typebars,
stubbled, a hail-struck

slice of inverted braille:
"The Trouble was by Design."

Clean script bound, he lifts
to feel the suture burn of sound

buckle. His men, turned against
work, unstitched labour's seam.

I lead my Fitzy for a jaunt to skein
elderly veins from the burst bladder
you highbrows still call Agassiz.
Shamed from my Karl stunt, I let
fingertips trick up one more ember-
bitten egg. Weather wraps cackleberry
in moss and seals it within a frayed
deer-rind sack. He negotiates plumes,
rides my gaunt S. We know sagging flags
are too heavy to sail. Swooned out, not
savouring what he hatched. Soot-egg
of dusk, a taste for fearpals, anoints
him and hands keys to the whammy.

I sashay as a winged-double, stalk
their brineboots, lope to Fitzy's gait,
and part feathers like greasy Frank,
but they're fire-blind to the fine time
I'm stewing. Frank whistles higher
octaves each day, marionette thoughts
twisted tighter by the smile. When
I hooked Zeus' moustache and
bent the handlebar behind his neck,
he lost his day face for night. I admit,
at dawn's yawn, the stooge will catch
you in shadow, but my new mirror
of mickle twins will shut them tight.

Wilhelmina, broken-teeth roads disappear when photo-graphs split by half-dash light, and make this quickening my permanent home. Peel back overburden, muskeg, glacial tills, sandstone and shale — useless turf-cutter's scraw — lie down in elephant drool like a swan that sinks into song. Wheels turn, I'm their undercarriage. I am, I am a gouge in a forest sea. Children with trowels excavate my flesh. They clutch feathers, demanding I give back the nest egg, I give back the oil wrapped in moss, the rotting moss beating in a deer-skin sack, the sack sewn in my chest, my chest bearing me tide to tide on river taunts, taunts that turn the wheel and reel me back into undercarriage, my only Wilhelmina. — RCF

Gentlemen, this script streamed from the lips of our dear premier: WHAT ALBERTA MAKES, MAKES ALBERTA. Do Not, I say, Do Not let this stain shade your eyes to the bulbous force of Pressure that is Backing our Spines toward the Pool's edge. Cowards gouge the threshold, vainly attempting to trip History. It's our Duty, our Burden, our Weight to drag them into the Future. Karl Clark: Traitor. Lloyd Champion: Scoundrel. Sidney Ells: Madman. Max Ball: Obscene. Jim Tanner: Bolshevik. Premier Manning: Purblind to what I've exhumed and sacrificed at his feet. Our Cause is our Own; we FACE Them Alone. No alarm, no panic, no despair. We have unearthed something that cannot be veiled again.

crickets squat
in my inner ear
too many tides
bear-hugging
the boiler's
squeal

my clock-chopped
mind mimes
the grind
for stumpy legs

I sit
think for hours
before I crush
sound out
of my head
with whiskey-water

Frank ferried the offering to my feet: casks of bent nails, bludgeoned license plates, window-screen skeps, panty-hose weather stripping, an unfurled trumpet, corner-slopped swallow's haunt, his thrumming hunger, sautéed rugs, an arrowhead, unopened letter from the Department of Mines, dynamite, cardboard kettles of staples, blanched bullet, and the scritch of his pains. A kitchen table was chewed by rain, and embers blistered the ground, my lonely Wilhelmina.
— RCF

Fitz shoots me
a skunk eye
says to double reef
each bolt tighter
doctor every wheel

handed me a bottle
of Perry Davis —
someone said
they drank
pitch as medicine

boy did we crack up

no sick days
till your swansong

boy did we hum along

Gentlemen, I tender evidence. Money-Men, perched in Darkness, watched The Film of Discovery wash over their bankrupt Faces. Tanner, Manning, Nielson, Champion, Maynard, Olafson, Stippleton, Lydera, Croft, Fallow, Turnman, Campbell — all Starving for Undeniable Proof. But it slipped out of reel, lapped, slapped, drawling out a Doodle Tongue while the Projectionist cursed Crabapples, cranking his Motor. No use: they rose, huddled, shrugged, and snapped lighters, laughing behind Turkey billows of smoke. Bodies Be Minds — Given — We must — Offer — I have Given and Give you — As I've told many times — Tide and Again. I know what One of You is Doing to Me. I know what you're After.

hopper has eyes too

birch skin gawks
rotten snows watch

Fitz everyplace
even in my night-trance

stop! tarring! my name!
in the hollow Commissary

refracting tower bird's-eye
cockeyes in the woods

and I dog-read a sole's crunch
counterfeiting my backtracks

Dust-ties-bootlaces Frank, spruce-tick-touch-river-swallowed Frank, needle-bloat limb-fringe Frank, shag-stream-mauled Frank, gouging-gable-planks Frank, sliming-clay-fines Frank, betrayed-barge-engine Frank, stalagmite-dentured pump-house Frank, hopper-blighted-with-leaves Frank, dead-straight-at-you-elephant-pool-eyes Frank, clenched-coot-skull Frank, fault-line-cheeks Frank, puckered-nails Frank, Commissary-bereft-of-elements Frank, capsized-Golden-Slipper Frank, rain-chewed-table Frank, swine-ration Frank, regurgitated-plant Frank, kingbird-butcher Frank, pollen-lust Frank, pledged-on-a-pin Frank, my last Wilhelmina. — RCF

Father would drill a ditty
of digging up seamy
swamp rocks

blubber'd I should never drown
down to the pits
keep lungs above veins

what would he jaw
spying me in this hotskull
doll'd in smut

pug mill hungry for my suspenders
camshaft grinding its tusks
pistons jab-stroking my guts

machines aspiring
to murder me
and Fitz whispering between fits

Carter Family visits
Jimmie Rodgers to tune-up
"T for Texas"

Maybelle imitates Brakeman's
yodel 'cause he's only got
one month left to breathe

worker bees
in my jug
their shrivelling
kidneys sour
each morning

silent Fitz —
he's brooding
an egg on
my platter
as rock doves
window-pout

each billy
counting snoozes

scuttle back to Waterways

Sunday's for kith rekindling, thus I
abdicate as industrial chaperone
and set a-strolling. Crusted barks sneer
at lattice moon sprout, squeeze out
sphagnum-rinds, and dune-bogs croak
as stomachs crest with fetid claw-tease;
blue spring's spruce in bristle-flex wind,
dementia and pluck along the pricked
river share, shiver shore, fettered trout-
spot trusses; craw-signed mud rustlers,
toppled balsam lisp, soil-wise shoots
slither, pollen snuff, birch-bugger red,
but too much Nature hurts my head.

Sweet Fitzy's dream-machines conspire
to shunt his shimmering schemes. I
smoke a rank cigar in his cabin, lick
photos of his wife — Wilhelmina's
a skin I would stay in — send her
billet-doux from Life in the North
("I'm sorry it's taken so long to peck").
Let's lay out instrument tables and
inventory our perversions: I wet for Frank
as much as the next hole. He's peeling
down the gown I wore on him
like earth. I've been inside you both,
but Frank's by far the finer soiler.

wilhelmina please wire fifty dollars to mcmurray bank STOP food shortage serious STOP already gone through supply of diesel oil STOP get some kind of barrels here on the double STOP advise if you can STOP come STOP could not pick worse time to show plant STOP seems acme of inconsistency STOP the swan eats my reports but wont let me STOP i dream the bears talk like frank STOP i guzzle coal soup STOP the egg fell from my chest STOP want to come home but i cant STOP worried STOP please STOP

Gentlemen, say there Is a louse that mines Inside a fish's jaw and sUcks Its tongue to A husk. The fiend Then stub-bolts and Acts the part, helping itself To sustenance while leaving Just enough for a usurped fingerling To keep afloat On. Nature's scoUrge within a home, And the chum-sucker unaware! Our Plant is No different: In Our ranks a louse syphOns for himself, upending balance and beauty of All we've done! When I find This vermin, I will squeeze Out the sum It's stolen from me and watch It dangle-drOwn in the court Of cUrrents.

sunday Plant's down

I pucker to my trombone
wind tongue motor
and feed all
a chew toe-back-ah shuffle

last night's nightdance

Fitz's sweat creeps up
lightning branches
then lets it rain
on ratchet dirt

Mother wish'd I'd been
a rockdoctor instead

5–1 cm, below
five shell buttons

How can this be the same man
riding a swan-horse —

third stage-left, flute erect,
an instrument-less orchestra.

How can this be the same barge
captain, as it sank, rig and crew

doomed. He bobs ashore, secures
new supplies, another dream team.

How the men tolerated him:
his clothes, his pitch, the war

between two photographs.
How the horse spooked from flute.

Fitz gibbering during mess
wouldn't dare my glare

my body-garb burn'd
in the boiler
my whiskey stash drain'd
feathers pluck'd from my cot

I line the floorboards
with lamp glass
a bear-snare for
predawn boot-tips

pillowcase sheathes
a busted bottleneck
to trace smiles
on his throat

Beneath tin-shy gibbous, I shimmered into bunkhouse. As he slept, I brewed before him: pounced, lashing hands, hurling clods of livid sand in his mask, biting fire eyes. For three tides I thundered a blade to his trunk, and three times no pain surfaced on Frank's craning form. Sizing up my rippling fist, I couldn't believe my pith had been stripped from beneath flesh. So I snared his tentacled mischief and choked throat with hammerstone, shrinking his thick neck, but when I peeled back layers of rotting rags, I found brittle feathers, no bulk beneath. His form had fled into elbow of night, leaving me a pupil in my palm, and I stole the cave of sleep, my fading Wilhelmina. — RCF

it wasn't machines choppin' me

Fitz-face humbles
his moon-horn brow
to mine so I taste
the heat of his panting

I rally glazed spurs
to cleave his shoulder

he double reefs
my scruff tighter
tears at sweat-stiff rags
and tricks out
my glass sight-bead

but I home-hammer
roller fists to fell
his tea-kettle

dog-crawl his guts out
bend a handle behind his neck
until he cashes
his day face for night

as gibbous flaps out my window

Fitzy and Frank thresh what I fed them,
flare their smokestack nostrils, but fail
to consummate the finale of blows.
I would ride those bodies down
river brains and heel-hang sense
into two billy brothers; would skim
their blood and do it all again with
a master's sprezzatura form; would
bestow myself mine own black egg,
and file the spoils inside a wake.
Their teeth, snug in the fist, to shave
planks, wood-skin piling at my feet:
useless, like scraw, this hired meat.

Surface
hacksaw blade fragment

Fitzsimmons puffed at Bitumount
for thirty years after shut in.

Caretaker allowed himself one
haircut per year, sentinelled the brink.

The shucked tin-husk betrays
a hopper brimming with leftovers.

Storage sheds regurgitate
salt-seeds eking over floorboards.

On the machine shop's door
he has mauled in blue paint,

"You will never never make it home
again if I catch you in this lab."

GentleFiends, investOrs have hOt-fOOted, ChampiOn has abandOned Us and Our hOmesteads, and all living strUctUres that walk Or swim Or fly Or creep Or wade Or scUttle are after Us, have rent the visiOn of NOrth we have wroUght. My Only Ointment is that the traitOr from within has been excreted — even a loUse mUst sleeptight. The stain Of Our bUrstheart is pUrged, and his fetid fabrications have dissipated intO bOreal's amnesiac wheeze. It may be tOO antiqUe, yOu are minOr fiends that must wOlf tO live, scroUnging back tO Waterways, bUt yoU'll never oUtbreak what we've Unearthed. YoU'll never be free of my UndertOw.

my baby toe
in water fits

backtrack my tracks
to McMurray

to spend a night-trance
on an abattoir floor

a fineline to find
train-whines
that crack
my ear bed

Surface
a letter from Wilhelmina

Through slants of pine bulls,
I hunt his log cabin, but prizes rot.

Bright felts limp on branches:
orange calls to ATVs, herding

home at dusk, as lichen blots
direction, its quickening bed.

"Robert, your every letter leaves
a soot print on my swan robe."

We jilt the spent excavation, stone
footings for the stove still standing.

Rollers in the distance are primed,
all else caught, overburdened.

Summary and Recommendations

I walk off my wedding ring,
slip it into a 25 cm strata sleeve.

Tobacco-feathered lungs struggle
to flap south, but my Mind-Swan

shackles me to the rebuild of His Cabin.
Fitzy demands much of me.

Tools simmer to surface, like this plane
and awl. Flaying planks for His Gloam Frame,

my legs drown in wood-skin waves.
Each beam is a pitch closer to scream,

Don't you dare ever come here, you'll be
beholding yourself bound to yourself in the tar cage.

As lamps dim on body boulevards,
I tender a trade: cheeks stained in lore,
toes palmated, face pin-fluffed, marred
lips billed, white flurry blinding shores
as last laughs are keyed from the locks.
Let us primp for hooded cameramen,
stuff mirrors with twins who mock
our crutched throats, blow carcinogens
out my breast, frying liquid air,
like pine seeds singed in fettered light
of a constellation's thighs, and dare
to ask, How was the fabricated flight?
Ah, but I know skin and bones are far
from their mad embrace without my tar.

Notes

The first epigraph is taken from Book XII of Ovid's *Metamorphoses*, translated by Allen Mandelbaum (New York: Harcourt, 1993), lines 222–226 in the English translation (pg. 403), lines 143–145 in the original Latin.

The second epigraph is from *The Truth About Alberta Tar Sands* (pg. 4), a pamphlet by Robert C. Fitzsimmons (Edmonton, AB: 1953).

The poem "Saw the new doc in McMurray today" (page 38) is indebted to Stanley Hoppenfeld's *Physical Examination of the Spine & Extremities.* (Norwalk, Connecticut: Appleton-Century-Crofts, 1976).

Several phrases and descriptions used in these poems were inspired by, or originated from, a variety of archival sources, including letters, telegrams, advertising pamphlets, photographs, company or archaeological reports, and personal histories. The narrative of *Tar Swan* is loosely based on the work of Robert C. Fitzsimmons and other early oil sands developers, but note that the events depicted are fictitious.

I consulted a number of oil sands history books while conducting research for these poems, but two in particular were very helpful: Barry Glen Ferguson's *Athabasca Oil Sands: Northern Resource Exploration, 1875–1951,* and Joyce Hunt's *Local Push — Global Pull.*

Acknowledgements

An early draft of this collection was completed with the assistance of a grant from the Alberta Foundation for the Arts.

Early versions of some of these poems were published in *The Malahat Review, The Fiddlehead, Grain, CV2,* and *Alberta Views.* As well, a selection from *Tar Swan* was awarded the 2014 CBC Poetry Prize and published in *enRoute* magazine. A brief excerpt from the poems was also included in *The Goods Lands: Canada Through the Eyes of Artists* (Figure 1 Publishing, 2017).

Composer Amy Brandon used portions of *Tar Swan* as the lyrics for her vocal-quartet composition *Gouging at a Forest S*ea, which premiered at Toronto's 21C Music Festival, in 2017.

For their support and encouragement over the years in working on this book, I owe many thanks to Kirk Miles, Bert Almon, Olga Costopoulos-Almon, Patrick Horner, Weyman Chan, Paul Marshall, and the Single Onion Poetry Series. Special thanks go out to my parents, Earl and Jane Martin.

As well, thanks to Robin Woywitka for providing technical input, for guiding me through the historic Bitumount site and several archeological dig sites, and for first introducing me to the work of Robert Fitzsimmons.

Thank you to Sandy Pool, Paul Zits, and Jeramy Dodds for your editorial assistance and advice. Also, a huge thanks to Jenna Butler, my editor at NeWest Press, for believing in my manuscript and helping to bring it out into the world. Thanks to Claire Kelly, Matt Bowes, and the rest of the team at NeWest for all their hard work with this book.

Most of all, I thank my wife, Marsha, for her love and support during the seemingly-endless trek of writing this book.

DAVID MARTIN was born and raised in Calgary, where he lives with his wife and children. His poetry has been awarded the CBC Poetry Prize, shortlisted for the Vallum Award for Poetry and PRISM international's poetry contest, and published in many journals and magazines across Canada. He is an instructor at The Reading Foundation, one of the organizers for Calgary's Single Onion poetry reading series, and the frontman for an indie-pop group, The Fragments.